E 457.6   Hanser, Richard.
.H3   Meet Mr. Lincoln, by Richard Hanser and Donald B.
           Hyatt. New York, Golden Press ₁1960₁

               131 p. illus. 28 cm.

               Adapted from the motion picture, Meet Mr. Lincoln, televised by
           the National Broadcasting Company as a Project twenty event on the
           150th anniversary of Lincoln's birth. Producer and director: Donald
           B. Hyatt. Script: Richard Hanser.

               1. Lincoln, Abraham, Pres. U. S.—Iconography.   I. Hyatt, Donald
           B. II. Meet Mr. Lincoln (Motion picture)

           E457.6.H3   923.173   59–15868 ‡

DISCARD

A Ridge Press Book / Golden Press, New York

MEET MR. LINCOLN

By Richard Hanser and Donald B. Hyatt

Project Twenty staff for
MEET MR. LINCOLN:

Producer and Director: DONALD B. HYATT
Script: RICHARD HANSER
Assistant Producer: ROBERT GARTHWAITE
Editor: SILVIO D'ALISERA
Assistant Editor: JOHN CHRISTOPHEL
Research: DANIEL W. JONES,
          RHODA GRADY, CHARLES OSBORN
Music: ROBERT RUSSELL BENNETT
Narration: ALEXANDER SCOURBY

SOURCES:

Ansco (Brady Collection) : 90 left.

Boston Public Library: 31 far right, 66.

Carpenter painting, U.S. Capitol: 69.

Chicago Historical Society: cover, 18 bottom, 22,
35, 40, 81 right, 121.

Dexter, Mrs. Byron: 34 top, 51, 104.

John Hay Library, Brown University: 127, 128-129, 131.

Jones, Daniel W.: 16-17, 18 top, 19, 60 bottom,
123, 124-125.

Knox College: 24, 25.

Laughlin, Clarence J.: 32-33.

Library of Congress: 12-13, 23 left, 28-29, 30-31,
38-39, 41, 49 bottom, 50 top, 53 top left & right,
57, 65 bottom, 74, 76-77, 83, 90 right, 91, 92-93, 94-95,
97, 100-101, 104-105, 109 (Brady Handy Collection),
110-111, 113, 114-115, 116-117, 120, 120-121.

Lincoln Collection of Boston University: 23 right.

Lincoln National Life Foundation: 6-7, 21, 80, 84 top.

Military Order of the Loyal Legion, Boston: 46-47.

Museum of the City of New York: 84 bottom, 112, 126, 132.

National Archives: 4-5, 15, 34 bottom, 37, 42-43, 48-49,
52 bottom, 53 bottom left & right, 54-55, 56, 60 top,
60-61, 62-63, 65 top, 67 left, 70-71, 72-73 bottom, 75,
78-79, 81 left, 82-83, 96, 102-103, 106-107, 122.

National Park Service: 58-59, 61 bottom, 73.

New York Historical Society: 8-9, 9, 10-11 top,
67 right, 85, 86 top left, 107, 118-119.

New York Public Library: 36, 44, 48, 86 bottom left,
86 right, 87, 89.

Public Library of Cincinnati: 10-11 bottom.

Rhode Island Historical Society: 14.

St. Louis Mercantile Society: 99.

Valentine Museum (Cook Collection) : 52 top, 64.

Virginia State Library: 50 bottom.

☀ Ridge Press:
Editor in chief: Jerry Mason
Editor: Adolph Suehsdorf
Art Director: Albert A. Squillace
Art Associate: Albert Kamp

Library of Congress Catalog Card Number: 59-15868

Prepared and produced by The
Ridge Press, Inc.
Printed in the United States of
America by Western Printing
and Lithographing Company.
Published by Golden Press, Inc.,
Rockefeller Center, New York 20,
New York.

FOREWORD

MEET MR. LINCOLN was conceived as a dramatic essay about
a man whose simplicity of being was the spirit of his greatness.
In our time, it is a greatness that travels the world, a spirit
that lives in distant places. Yet, in America, something has
happened to the Lincoln legend, something has passed away.
A kind of pleasant myth has sapped the strength of an exciting
reality. Perhaps it is because we in America, in childlike
innocence, have too eagerly accepted Lincoln in godlike terms,
or perhaps it is because, in adult pride, we have ignored the
person in order to create a proud image on a towering pedestal,
obscured in wispy clouds of blind allegiance. Whatever—the
beauty of Lincoln has too often been colored by the cloak of
complexity.

To be sure, Lincoln was a man of wondrous depth, of warm love
and craggy manner, of slow, brilliant reasoning and quick,
hand-hewn philosophy, of softness and hardness, and in appearance
a paradox, a beautiful ugliness that was poetry in expression.

He was a man loved and hated for the same thing at the same time.
He was all the things that men are, and if there is any mystery
about the man Lincoln, it is because he was infinitely human.
That was his greatness and his genius, created from a thousand
complexities, but molded into a oneness of purpose.

Our story is about that oneness. It is a story that is told with
a freshness and simplicity that captures the essence of Lincoln.
And by a blending of pictures and words, the story is told in a
new and dramatic manner, with a sweep of history such as no text
or picture book alone could do.

MEET MR. LINCOLN was televised by the National Broadcasting
Company—and sponsored by the Lincoln National Life Insurance
Company—as a Project Twenty event on the 150th anniversary of
Lincoln's birth. Richard Hanser's text, which has been described
as a kind of "graphic poetry," draws largely upon Lincoln's own
words. The pictures, selected by Daniel W. Jones and his
assistants from 25,000 photographs, daguerreotypes, and prints,
were gathered from archives and private collections throughout
the country. They are a unique heritage of America, illuminating
powerfully human moments of history that no words could describe.
We can thank Matthew Brady, Alexander Gardner, Alexander Hesler,
and many unknowns for these riches.

On the following pages, MEET MR. LINCOLN is faithfully
preserved for leisurely study; through the highlighting of
historical events that are the backdrop for the drama of Lincoln,
we feel that you will truly MEET MR. LINCOLN.

Donald B. Hyatt
Producer-director, MEET MR. LINCOLN

Washington in November of 1860:
an uneasy city awaits a newly elected President,
and in the still unfinished dome of
the Capitol some see a sign of the times—

"unfinished, like the Union itself."

It is a bustling time, a thriving
country. But the President-elect
himself has called this America
"a house divided." Other voices speak
even more ominously: "We live
in the midst of strong agitations
and we are surrounded by
very considerable dangers to our
institutions and government."
For thirty-one million Americans,
a turning point has come.

All across the country now, eyes
turn toward the American heartland,
toward the President-elect.
Many are asking:
What do we know of him but that "he was
born in the wilds of Kentucky and
reared in the wilds of Indiana and Illinois?"
His campaign song had gone:
Old Abe Lincoln came

Out of the wilderness,
Out of the wilderness
Down in Illinois.

The "Rail Splitter" candidate, the
campaigners called him,
the "backwoodsman."
But who is this Lincoln? You must
travel to a place called Springfield to
find out. They know him there.

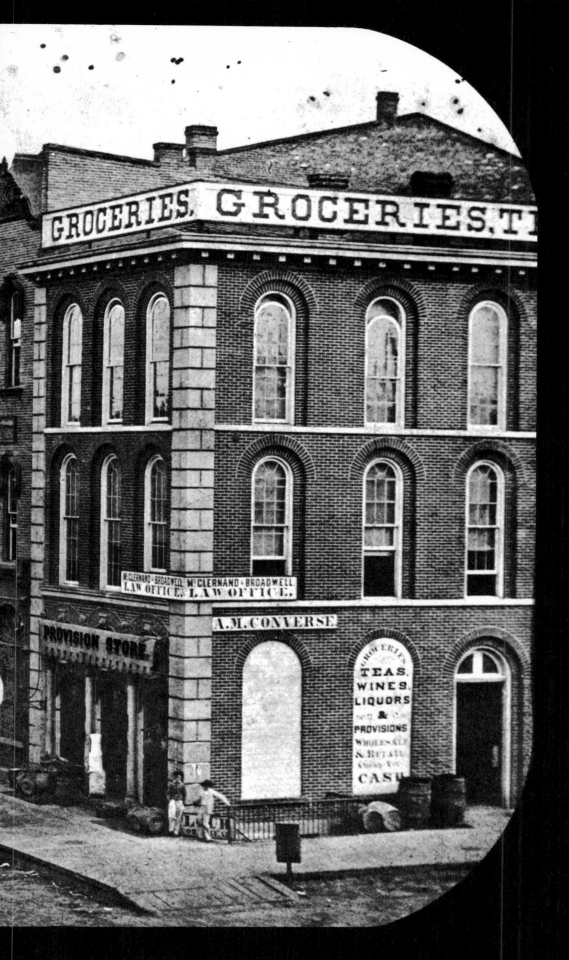

He started out,
in his own words,
as "a strange,
friendless,
uneducated,
penniless boy,"
but there he grew
and developed
at a time
and place
of great growth
and development.

Through a quarter-century, they watched his rise:
from self-taught lawyer to a force
in State politics, and trustee of his adopted town.
Now the people have called him from Springfield to face
a task which, as he tells his fellow-townsmen,
is "greater than that which rested on George Washington."

He has come a
far journey
from the log cabin
of his backwoods
birth to this
comfortable home —

the home of a successful
provincial lawyer and politician.
But for America the question persists:
Is he more than that?
Is there something deeper?

There is.

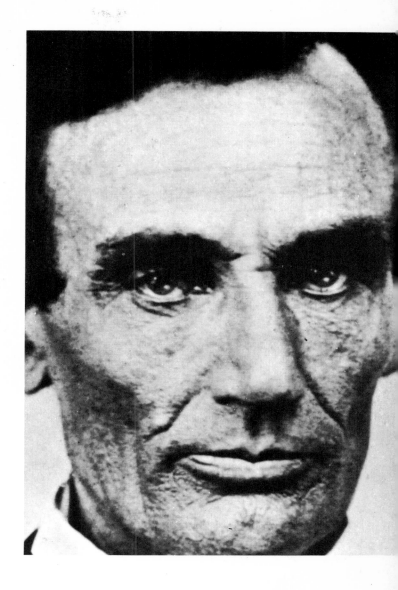

As a State legislator and
Congressman, as a searching,
probing student of democracy
and its workings, he
slowly, quietly ripened
and deepened through the years.
When great national issues
challenged him, he was ready.

His great debates with "The Little
Giant"—Senator Stephen A. Douglas—
in 1858 "set the prairies on fire"
and spread his name across the country.
Listeners felt something "elemental and
mystical" in his speeches of "unyielding
hostility" to the spread of slavery
into the new territories of the West.
As "the prophetic man of the present,"
the new Republican Party made him
its presidential candidate. Now,
as President-elect, his position
remains unchanged: "On the question of
extending slavery, I am inflexible."

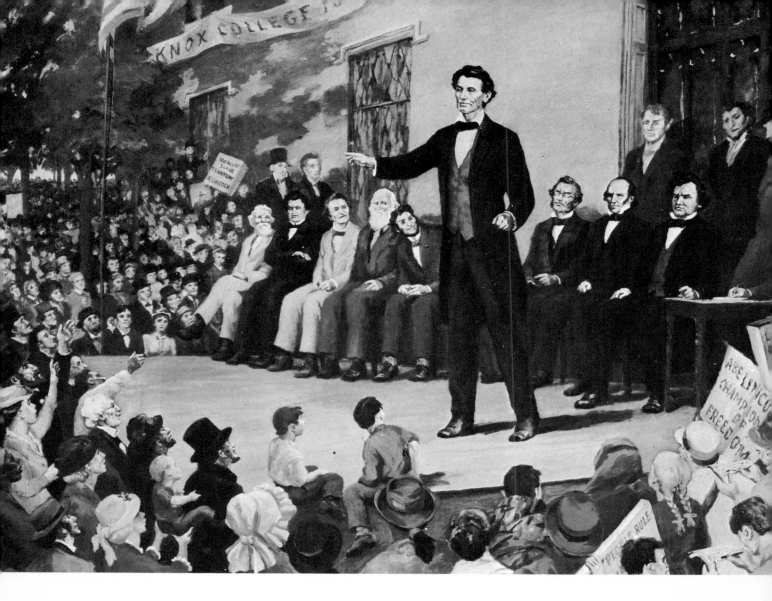

$1200 TO 1250 DOLLARS! FOR NEGROES!!

THE undersigned wishes to purchase a large lot of NEGROES for the New Orleans market. I will pay $1200 to $1250 for No. 1 young men, and $850 to $1000 for No. 1 young women. In fact I will pay more for likely

NEGROES,

Than any other trader in Kentucky. My office is adjoining the Broadway Hotel, on Broadway, Lexington, Ky., where I or my Agent can always be found.

WM. F. TALBOTT.

LEXINGTON, JULY 2, 1853.

Where the "peculiar institution" already exists,
Abraham Lincoln intends no interference
by the Government. He favors "toleration
by necessity." But in the South his election seems
a menace to the very survival of an
agrarian society based on the labor of some
three million slaves, to a system long sanctioned
by custom and the Constitution. And the South remembers
another Lincoln saying and deeply distrusts
him for it: "I believe this Government cannot
endure permanently half slave and half free."

Long ago the prediction was made: "Sir, slavery will not be overthrown

without excitement, a most tremendous excitement.'' So it proves.

All through the South the tremor runs,
the convulsion of a once-serene society that
feels itself threatened with extinction.

33

In Charleston, South Carolina
—in December of 1860—
the fabric of the Union,
long strained in the violent
tug-of-war between North and
South, is torn asunder.
In Institute Hall, where men
shout, ''Resistance to Lincoln
is obediance to God!''
an Ordinance of
Secession declares South
Carolina a ''separate and
independent State.''

South Carolina.

At a Convention of the People of the State of South Carolina, begun and holden at Columbia, on the Seventeenth day of December, in the year of our Lord one thousand eight hundred and Sixty, and thence continued by adjournment to Charleston, and there by divers adjournments to the Twentieth day of December in the Same year —

"dissolve the Union between the State of South Carolina and other States united with her under the compact entitled *d States of America*"

uth Carolina, in Convention assembled, do declare and ordain, and it is hereby declared and ordained, That the Ordinance adopted twenty-third day of May, in the year of our Lord One thousand Seven hundred and eighty-eight, whereby the Constitution of the United d, and also all Acts and parts of Acts of the General Assembly of this State, ratifying amendments of the said Constitution, are here on now subsisting between South Carolina and other States, under the name of "The United States of America," is hereby dissolved.

Done at Charleston, the twentieth day of December, in the year of our Lord one thousand eight hundred and Sixty

D. F. Jamison — Delegate from Barnwell and President of the Convention.

les Perrin Francis Hugh Wardlaw Chesley D. Evans R. W. Barnwell J. W. Spratt
Noble R. G. M. Dunovant Wm. W. Harllee Jos. Dan'l Pope Williams Middleton
n James Parsons Carroll A. W. Bethea C. P. Brown H. D. Thompson
son Wm. Gregg E. W. Goodwin John McKingler B. H. Rutledge
Wardlaw Andrew J. Hammond William D. Johnson Daniel D. DuBy Edward McCrady
Calhoun James Tompkins Alex. McLeod A. Mazyck Francis S. Porcher
Middleton James C. Smyly John P. Kinard Williams Cain I. L. Gowdin
E. Sessions John Hugh. Means Robert Moorman P. G. Snowden John S. Palmer
Tiler William Strother Lyles Joseph Caldwell Geo. W. Seabrook John LeNowell
Orr Henry Campbell Davis Simeon Fair John Jenkins John S. O'Hear
eed Jno. Buchanan Thomas Worth Glover R. I. Davant John G. Landrum
mpson James C. Furman Laurence M. Hett E. M. Seabrook B. B. Foster
Duncan Donald Rowe Barton John E. Wannamaker Benjamin F. Kilgore
H. Easley Wm. Hunter Elias B. Scott Jas. H. Carlisle
Harrison Andrew F. Lewis Jos. E. Jenkins Simpson Bobo
ampbell Witt H. Thompson Langdon Cheves Wm. Curtis
Withers William S. Grisham George Rhodes J. H. Green
Chesnut John Maxwell A. J. Shahala Matthew P. Mayrey
Brevard Kershaw Jno. E. Frampton Wm. Porcher Miles Thomas Reese, English Jr.
W. Beaty W. Ferguson Hutson John Townsend Albertus Chambers Spain
Eller W. F. de Saussure Robert C. Gourdin H. W. Gadberry
Crawford William Hopkins F. W. Conner H. Davis
authier James H. Adams Theodore D. Wagner Wm. H. Lest
Robinson Maxcy Gregg R. Barnwell Rhett James Jefferies
Young John H. Kinsler C. G. Memminger Anthony W. Dozier
Gaillington Ephraim M. Clark Gabriel Manigault John C. Restley
Williams Alex. H. Brown John Julius Pringle Smith R. C. Logan
Watts E. S. P. Bellinger Isaac W. Hayne Francis S. Parker
Tyler Merrick E. Carn Jno. H. Honour Benj'n Funeral Dunkin
ghman E. R. Henderson Rich'd De Treville Sam'l Taylor Atkinson
Geiger Peter Stokes Tho. Jno. Hanckel Alex'r M. Forster
Wilson Paul Quattlebaum Daniel Flud A. W. Burnet Wm. Blackburn Wilson
Timmons W. B. Rowell David C. Appleby Thos. J. Simons Robert T. Allison
Artemas J. Darby Sam'l Rainey
A. Baxter Springs
A. J. Barron

F. Arthur Clerk of the Convention.

The following February—even
before Lincoln can be inaugurated
—six other states join
the movement. In Montgomery, Alabama,
the Confederate States of America
are founded. Their President:
the former Secretary of War,
Jefferson Davis of Mississippi.

T

UN

I

DISS

E

ON

LVED!

Abraham Lincoln, aged 52,
sixteenth American President:
bearded now, and somber, on this
somber Inauguration Day—March
the 4th, 1861. Almost his
opening words are a reassurance
to the South that he intends
no action against its "property,
peace, and security." And, as
he pleads for calmness and
forbearance, he stresses two of
his deepest convictions. He says:
"I hold that the Union
of these States is perpetual."

And he asks: "Why should there not be a patient confidence
in the ultimate justice of people? Is there any
better or equal hope in the world?"
"In your hands, my dissatisfied fellow countrymen, and not
in mine, is the momentous issue of civil war.
The Government will not assail you. You can have no
conflict, without being yourselves the
aggressors. You have no oath registered in Heaven
to destroy the Government, while I shall have
the most solemn one to 'preserve, protect, and defend' it!"

But now a crisis quickly looms that no eloquence
can soothe or diminish: Fort Sumter in
Charleston Harbor, symbol to the North of the
Federal authority that must be maintained
if the flag is not to become "the hiss and scoff of
the world." For the South, Sumter is
a symbol of domination by a "foreign" power, an
intolerable affront to the sovereignty
of an independent State. The North will not withdraw;
the South acts.

April 13th, 1861: Fort Sumter surrenders.
A reporter writes: "The curtain has fallen on
Act One of the great tragedy of the age."

WAR!
AT LAST

TO ARMS!
To Arms! To Arms!
Defend your Homes and Firesides.

A young Northerner, who speaks
for thousands North and South, exults:
"The greatness of the crisis, the
Homeric grandeur of the contest, surrounds
and elevates us all." So the Civil War
begins, with high-flown rhetoric...

with picture-book poses.

"So large an army as the Government now has
on foot," says Abraham Lincoln, "was never known
before, without a soldier in it but has
taken his place there of his own free choice."

But for months after Fort
Sumter, there is no major fighting.
War seems an agreeable routine.
An Illinois recruit writes home:
"I never enjoyed anything
in the world as I do this life."

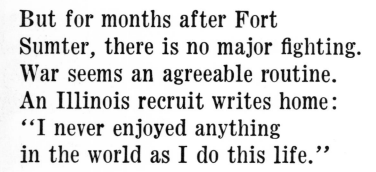

"The people think there is a royal road to
peace," says Abraham Lincoln. "They have no idea
that the war is to be carried out and put through
by hard, tough fighting that will hurt somebody..."
And in the South, a General
named Nathan Bedford Forrest says:
"War means fighting.
And fighting means killing."

"This great trouble," Lincoln calls it, and mounting
defeat, mounting casualties, wring from him a despairing:
"My God! My God! What will the country say?"

Long and hard he searches for a general to match
the military genius who is leading the South to victory
after victory over the numerically superior North,
a general to match Robert Edward Lee of Virginia, called
"the grandest figure on any field." And
second only to Lee in dash and brilliance is his strong
right arm, General Stonewall Jackson.
"It is called the Army of the Potomac," says Lincoln,
"but it is only McClellan's bodyguard."

General-in-Chief George McClellan has
organized a powerful striking force,
but hesitates to strike; he falters, waits. Says
the President: "He has got the slows."
"Delay is ruining us." McClellan cavalierly
brushes aside the President's counsel, but Lincoln
is patient: "I will hold McClellan's horse
if he will only bring us success."

But instead of successes, the new Military
Telegraph clicks out: heavier casualties,
more retreat. Black bulletins pour into the
War Department in Washington
where Abraham Lincoln reads the dispatches and
broods upon their larger meanings.
"The struggle of today," he says, "is not
altogether for today. It is for a vast future also."

To Lincoln, the enduring Union of a free
people in this free, expanding land is
"the last, best hope of earth." The whole war is
a testing whether his countrymen shall
"nobly save, or meanly lose" this last, best hope—
democracy's future, America's future. "The dogmas of
the quiet past," he says, "are inadequate
to the stormy present. The occasion is piled high
with difficulty, and we must rise with the
occasion. As our case is new, so we must think
and act anew. We must disenthrall
ourselves, and then we shall save our country."
And he rises with the occasion by giving
the war a higher significance, a deeper purpose.
In midsummer of 1862, he presents to his
Cabinet the draft of an Emancipation Proclamation.
He will strengthen the cause of the Union
by freeing the slaves. But the Cabinet cautions,
the Proclamation can have little force or effect
if issued amid continuing Union disaster.

And then it comes:
a Union victory—one of the
bloodiest days of the war,
when Lee's advance into Maryland
is checked at the battle of
Antietam, with appalling casualties
on both sides.
Now the first phase of emancipation
can be proclaimed to the world
as "an act of justice, warranted
by the Constitution
upon military necessity."

"In giving freedom to the slave,"
says Abraham Lincoln, "we assure freedom to
the free—honorable alike in what
we give, and what we preserve." For him,
the Emancipation Proclamation is
"the central act of my administration, and the
great event of the Nineteenth Century."

one thousand eight hundred
and sixty three, and of the
Independence of the United
States of America the eighty-
seventh.

Abraham Lincoln

By the President.

William H. Seward,
Secretary of State.

73

They have builded Him an altar
in the evening dews and damps;
I have seen Him in the watch fires
of a hundred circling camps...
As the war goes on, the Battle Hymn
of the Republic sings of it as
a crusade, a noble mission.
As He died to make men holy,
let us die to make men free.

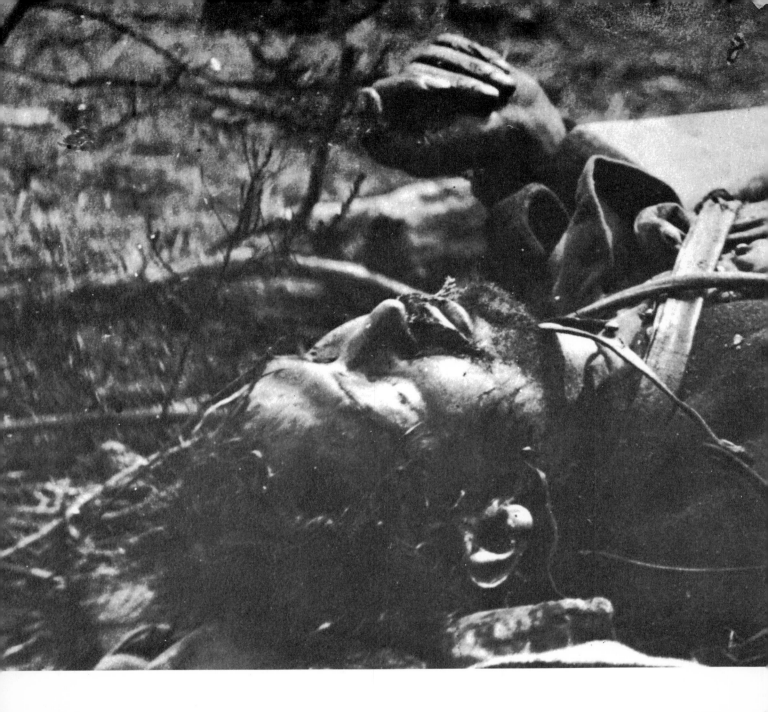

But Lincoln's thoughts are with the soldiers—
the men of Fredericksburg and Chancellorsville,
of Vicksburg and Gettysburg—when he says:
"This war of ours, in its magnitude and duration,
is one of the most terrible...it has carried
mourning into almost every home, until it can almost be
said that the 'Heavens are hung in black.'"

Gettysburg, Pennsylvania, on November 19th, 1863.
A cemetery is being dedicated, a burial ground for 6,000
soldiers, North and South, who fell here
last July; parades and speeches now, where once
the Union line broke Pickett's Charge.
For two hours the crowds are spellbound by the classic
oratory of the greatest speaker of his day,
Edward Everett, diplomat and scholar. The President's
speech is secondary. He has been asked to
make only "a few appropriate remarks."

But in his words the meaning of Gettysburg—of the war itself—is caught for all time: "...that from these honored dead we take increased devotion to that cause for which they gave the last full measure of devotion—that we here highly resolve that these dead shall not have died in vain—that this nation, under God, shall have a new birth of freedom—and that government of the people, by the people, for the people, shall not perish from the earth."
The speech evokes little interest. Lincoln thinks it a failure.

In the privacy of a White House
sometimes threatened by Confederate capture,
a wearied President must find what
relief he can. His chief delight is his
little Tad, whom he habitually
pampers and spoils. "But," says Lincoln, "his
brother Bob was just such a little
rascal, and now he is a very decent boy."

The First Lady—
Mary Todd Lincoln—an
adoring wife, but
emotionally unstable,
overly fond of
extravagance and display.
She shines at White
House balls and
levees where the President
is awkward and
uncomfortable. He
much prefers to
meet people informally,
to learn what they
think and say.

But midway in 1864, the
political talk is that Lincoln
will not, cannot be re-elected. The war
drags on, the casualties multiply.
Who is to blame?
The President.

Says Lincoln: "If there is a
worse place than Hell, I am in it."
With the South still undefeated,
the North itself falls prey to rampant
disloyalty and violent dissension,
as in the savage New York
draft riots of the year before.
Bitter political antagonisms well up,
and Abraham Lincoln is vilified
and mocked in the press as no other
President has ever been.
They call him "clown" and "fiend,"
a laughing stock, "the Illinois beast."

I WISH I WERE IN DIXIE

But the people are not misled.
As Lincoln says: "Truth is generally
the best vindication against slander."
And the people keep their faith in him,
the soldiers win him timely victories;
the election vindicates him.

LONG ABRAHAM
A LITTLE LONGER

"I am a slow walker, but I never
walk back." And now at last
the pace quickens toward the goal
he so deeply yearns for: peace and Union.
By now he has not only the troops,
but he has found the man to lead
them: Ulysses S. Grant, who conquered
Vicksburg and split the Confederacy.
"I can't spare this man," says Lincoln.
"He fights."
And so does William Tecumseh Sherman,
who says: "War is cruelty
and you cannot refine it."

After more than three years of Civil War, Lincoln is able to tell the country: "We are not exhausted...we are gaining strength." The factories of the industrial North send mounting masses of new weapons to the fronts, while the Confederacy—blockaded, bled white of men and supplies—fights on nerve alone.

No longer can the rapier of
Robert Lee fend off the battering-ram
of Grant and Sherman from
the citadels of the South: Atlanta...
Savannah...Charleston...
Richmond itself.
As Robert Lee has said:
"It is well that war is so terrible,
or we should become too fond of it."
With half a million dead,
North and South, America, at last,
has its fill of war.

Palm Sunday. The great stillness comes
at Appomattox, in Virginia. After four years
of unequal struggle, the South
surrenders. The arms are stacked.

And a Union general,
Joshua Chamberlain of the 20th Maine
—remembering—pays tribute
to the soldiers of the Confederacy:
"Before us in proud humiliation stood
the embodiment of manhood:
Men whom neither toils nor sufferings,
nor the fact of death, nor
disaster, nor hopelessness could
bend from their resolve:
Standing before us now, thin, worn and
famished, but erect, with eyes looking
level into ours, waking memories that
bound us together as no other bond—
Was not such manhood to be welcomed back
into a Union so tested and assured... ?
How could we help falling on our
knees, all of us together, and praying
God to pity and forgive us all!"

2d Edition.

LEE SURRENDERS

Glory to God in the Highest :

Peace on Earth, Good will

Amongst Men.

April 14th, Good Friday: All Washington basks in victory's afterglow, and the President shares the mood this day. "We are going to have good times now, and a united country," he tells a White House visitor. Now his one wish is to "bind up the nation's wounds"—"with malice toward none, with charity for all."

In late afternoon, he and Mary go for a
carriage ride through the city,
and he speaks cheerfully of their future:
a trip to Europe perhaps, when his term
is over, and then—quiet years
again in Springfield. But now, today, with
"the great trouble" past,
"I never felt so happy," he says.

This evening he and Mary are going to the theatre—Ford's Theatre. It has been in the papers that the President will attend. The whole town knows it.

FORD'S THEATRE
TENTH STREET, ABOVE E.

SEASON II .... WEEK XXXI .... NIGHT 196
WHOLE NUMBER OF NIGHTS, 495

JOHN T. FORD...PROPRIETOR AND MANAGER
(Also of Holliday St. Theatre, Baltimore, and Academy of Music, Phil'a.)
Stage Manager..J. B. WRIGHT
Treasurer..H. CLAY FORD

Friday Evening, April 14th, 1865

LAST NIGHT
OF MISS
LAURA KEENE
THE DISTINGUISHED MANAGERESS, AUTHORESS AND ACTRESS,
Supported by
JOHN DYOTT and HARRY HAWK

TOM TAYLOR'S CELEBRATED ECCENTRIC COMEDY,
As originally produced in America by Miss Keene, and performed by her upwards of

ONE THOUSAND NIGHTS,
ENTITLED
OUR AMERICAN
COUSIN

FLORENCE TRENCHARD	MISS LAURA KEENE

(Her original character.)

Abel Murcott, Clerk to Attorney	John Dyott
Asa Trenchard	Harry Hawk
Sir Edward Trenchard	T. C. GOURLAY
Lord Dundreary	E. A. EMERSON
Mr. Coyle, Attorney	J. MATTHEWS
Lieutenant Vernon, R. N.	W. J. FERGUSON
Captain De Boots	C. BYRNES
Binney	G. W. PEAR
Buddicomb, a valet	J. L. STAND
John Whicker, a gardener	J. L. DE BONAY
Bailiffs	G. A. PARKHURST and L. JOHNSON
Mary Trenchard	Miss J. GOURLAY
Mrs. Mountchessington	Mrs. H. MUZZY
Augusta	Miss. H. TRUEMAN
Georgiana	Miss M. HART
Sharpe	Mrs. J. H. EVANS
Skillet	Miss M. GOURLAY

PATRIOTIC SONG AND CHORUS
"HONOR TO OUR SOLDIERS."

Honor to our soldiers,
Our nation's greatest pride,
Who, neath our Starry Banner's folds,
Have fought, have bled and died ;
They 're nature's noblest handiwork—
No King so proud as they.
God bless the heroes of the land,
And cheer them on their way."

Words by H. B. Phillips; Music Composed and Arranged by Prof. William
Withers, Jr.; Solos by Miss M. Hart, H. B. Phillips and George M. Arth,
and the Ladies and Gentlemen of the Company.

SATURDAY EVENING, APRIL 15,

BENEFIT of Miss JENNIE GOURLAY
When will be presented BOURCICAULT'S Great Sensation Drama,
THE OCTOROON

And so does an actor named John Wilkes Booth.
Feverishly romantic, insanely vain,
he has appointed himself avenging angel for the
South's defeat, and enlisted...

a band of conspirators—
deserters, mental defectives, thugs—
in a plot
against the Government.

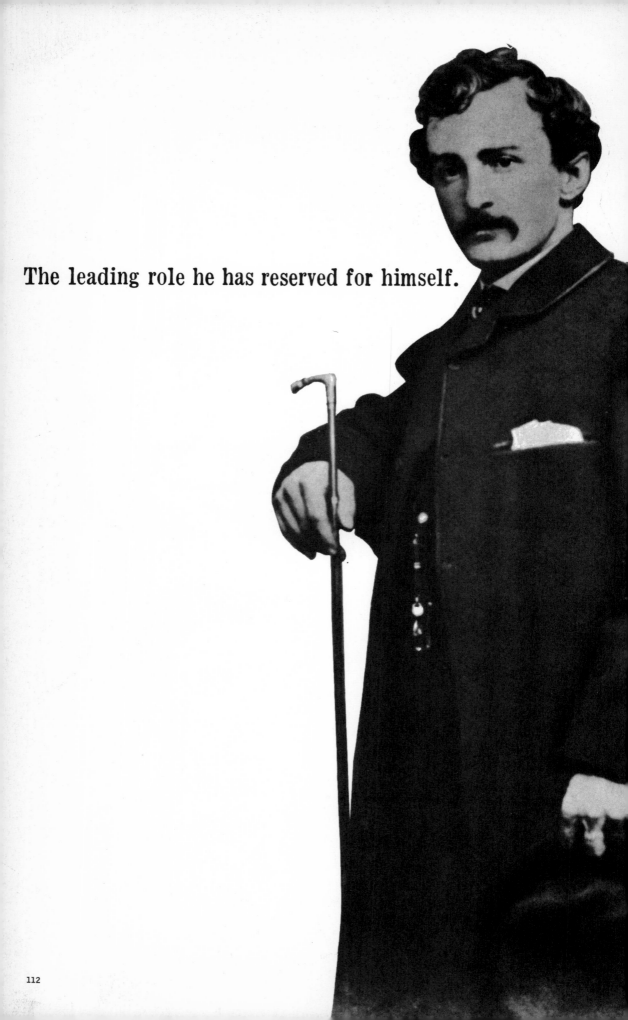

The leading role he has reserved for himself.

he will assassinate the President.

The President is disinclined
to attend the theatre this
evening, but he has promised his
wife and he does not
wish to disappoint the people.
"It is the kind of engagement
I never break," he says.

"Ever thus to tyrants!"
shouts the assassin as he flees.

A doctor from the audience examines
the President's wound. "It is mortal," he says.
"He cannot recover."
Six soldiers carry him unconscious into
the night, across Tenth Street,
to a boarding house where the nearest
empty bed can receive him.
In the house of strangers, at the end
of a strange corridor, Abraham Lincoln
finds the end of his road.

Now all that has ever been said against him recedes

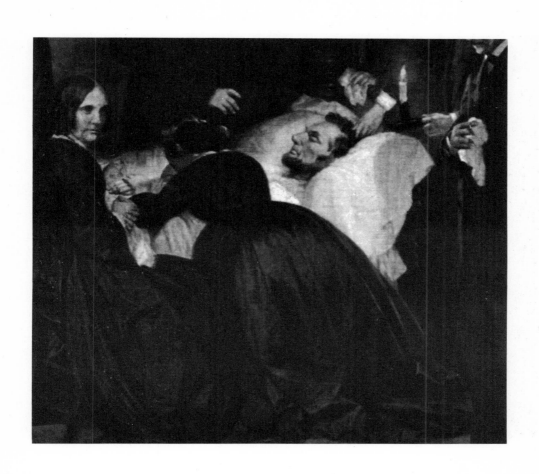

and fades, and men begin to remember the other words:

"the greatest sign and marvel of our day—a plain
man of the people called to conduct the passage of a great
people through a crisis involving the destinies of
the whole world." That has been said of him.
"He was Heaven's instrument to conduct his people
through a Red Sea of blood to a Canaan of peace and freedom."
That has been said of him.

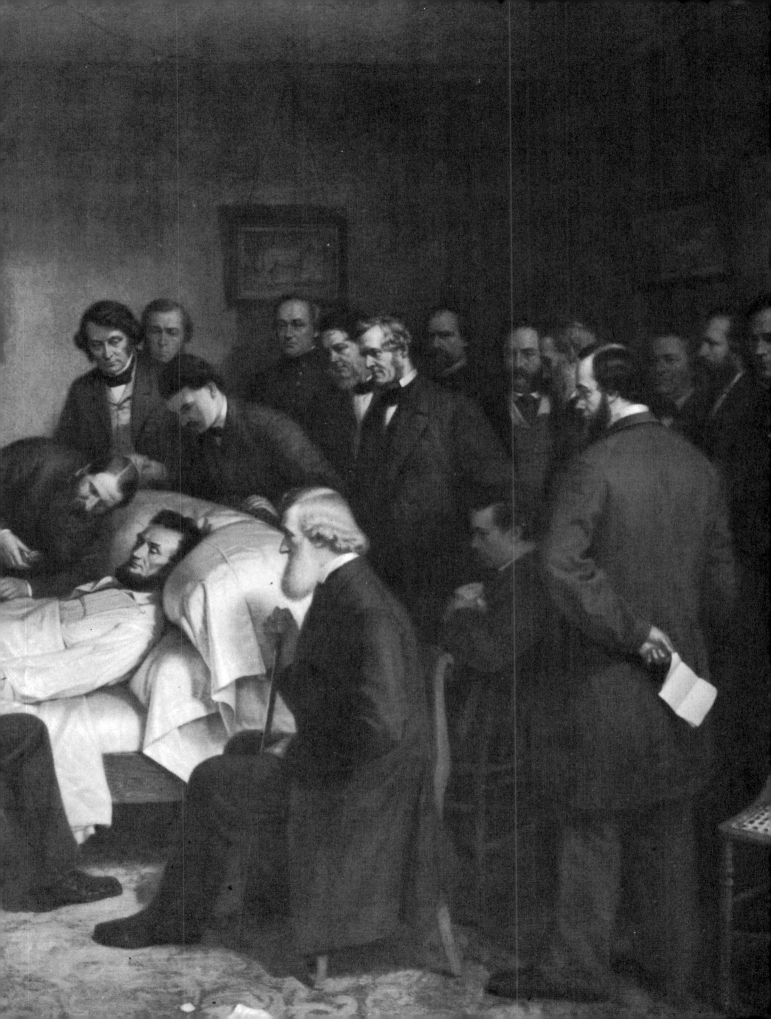

Once, during the war, when he was urged to rest, to ease his burden, he had answered: "The tired part of me is inside and out of reach." Now his rest will be long.